How to
Find
Follow
Fulfill
God's Will

Andrew Wommack

© Copyright 2024 – Andrew Wommack

Printed in the United States of America. All rights reserved. No portion of this book may be reproduced, stored in a retrieval system, or transmitted in any form or by any means—electronic, mechanical, photocopy, recording, scanning, or other—except for brief quotations in critical reviews or articles, without the prior written permission of the publisher.

Unless otherwise indicated, all Scripture quotations are taken from the King James Version® of the Bible. Copyright © by the British Crown. Public domain.

Published by Andrew Wommack Ministries, Inc.
Woodland Park, CO 80863

ISBN 13 TP: 978-1-59548-732-2

For Worldwide Distribution, Printed in the USA

1 2 3 4 5 6 / 27 26 25 24

Contents

Introduction 1
'You're the One!' 2
God Knows You 4
A Living Sacrifice 6
Let Peace Rule 9
Renew Your Mind 11
You Choose 13
Holy Dissatisfaction 15
The Desires of Your Heart 17
Steps and Stages 19
Exercise Patience 22
A Place Called There 24
Course Correction 26
Timing Is Everything 29
Your Spirit Knows 31
Unravel the Mystery 34
Get the Interpretation 36
Don't Quit 39
Keep At It 41
Run Your Race 43
Keep Your Eyes on Jesus 46
Conclusion 48
Receive Jesus as Your Savior 51
Receive the Holy Spirit 53

Introduction

Do you ever wonder why God put you on this earth? Are you seeking to find purpose and be a blessing to others? Do you want to discover God's calling for your life but don't know where to start?

God's will for your life is never going to be the easy thing to do. It's going to be something you have to pursue. If you don't pursue it, you won't fulfill it. God has a purpose for every single one of you, and it's only when you discover that purpose that you will really find true satisfaction, joy, and peace.

I believe God has a perfect plan for every single person. I know that based on the Word of God, and that's what I'm going to share in this booklet. I also know that most people are not really doing what God has called them to do. They let circumstances control them and push them in any direction. They behave like water, always seeking the lowest level and the path of least resistance.

Some of you are seeking the Lord and are still dissatisfied. One of the reasons you feel that way is because you aren't in that spot that God has for you. There is such a thing as holy dissatisfaction, which is one way God motivates you toward fulfilling His will. You won't find true happiness, peace, and satisfaction until you are in the center of God's will.

'You're the One!'

I went to Charlotte, North Carolina, for more than thirty years to minister at a certain church. I built a lot of relationships there, including one with a partner who owned a business with about three dozen employees.

This man would invite me to speak to his staff every year when I came to town. He would tell them, "The clock's running. You just listen to this guy as long as he wants to talk. I'm paying you." So, I would minister to his employees from what God had shown me in His Word, and after it was over I'd go to the breakroom and pray with people. We saw lots of people saved and healed, and miracles happened. It was really good!

One year when I went there, I walked out after ministering to people and an Asian woman was sitting at the front desk. I hadn't seen her with the rest of the group, so I said, "Who are you?" Once she told me her name, I asked, "Why weren't you back with the rest of the employees?" This woman said, "I'm the 'new kid on the block' and they left me here to answer the phones."

We kept on talking, and at some point, she asked, "What do you do?" So, I said, "I'm a minister." When I said that, her eyes got really big. Then she asked, "For who?" And I said, "For the Lord Jesus Christ!" That's when she looked at me and said, "You're the one!" And all I could say was, "I'm 'the one' what?"

This woman told me that she was a Buddhist, and the previous night she had been going through her rituals. She said she just stopped right in the middle of it all and said, "God, I know You exist, but this can't be it." She had a sincere desire to know who God really was, so she said, "Reveal Yourself to me."

She said that a ball of light appeared in front of her, and it was pulsating. As this woman looked at it, she heard a voice say, "Tomorrow, I will send you a man who will tell you who I am."

That's when she said to me again, "You're the one!" And I responded, "I'm the one!" I got to lead that lady to the Lord and prayed with her to receive the Baptism of the Holy Spirit right there! And as joyous as that was to see her life change, when I got to my car, I just had to sit there for a while, praising the Lord.

I was thinking, *God, I was in the right place at the right time*. I was right in the center of His will. He knew I'd be there, and I got to be "the one" when that woman cried out to God asking Him to reveal Himself.

Now that's a feeling of satisfaction you will never get doing your own thing and asking God to bless it. That thought deep in your heart that there must be something more to life than this is probably the Lord speaking to you and trying to move you toward His divine plan for your life.

God Knows You

Thine eyes did see my substance, yet being unperfect; and in thy book all my members were written, which in continuance were fashioned, when as yet there was none of them.

Psalm 139:16

God saw you before you were ever born. He saw you in your mother's womb. While you were being physically formed, God wove in your talents, abilities, and purpose. It's a part of who you are. Before you were even born, God had already written down what your life is supposed to be. He had written down your talents and abilities.

There is no such thing as a self-made man or woman. You can't bring out what God didn't put in. God gave you a disposition. He gave you a certain inclination. God made you the way you are. You can change to a degree, but you can't change the core of who you are.

I used to be a runner, but now I'm a walker. I may walk up to five miles a day. But in high school, they tried to make me run sprints over short distances up to 440 yards. I did it, but I hated it and was never really good at it. I was good enough to make the track team, but never good enough to win any medals.

After I finished school, I started jogging and discovered that I loved to jog. I enjoyed running fifteen or twenty miles slowly, but running short distances as fast as I could really bothered me. I eventually learned that muscles are made up of fast-twitch and slow-twitch fibers.

Sprinters have a majority of fast-twitch muscle fibers, while distance runners have more slow-twitch muscle fibers. You can change the ratio of fast-twitch to slow-twitch fibers in your muscles through training, but not by much. The basic balance doesn't change. Some people are built for speed while others are built for endurance.[1] I didn't like sprinting because I wasn't built to run sprints. I was built for long-distance running.

In the same way, your personality can be influenced and changed to a degree, but you have a disposition to be a certain type of person. You were designed that way. Before you were formed, God had already planned those things.

God created you with a purpose. The Lord knows everything about you and has even determined what your life is supposed to be. In my life, God ordained that I be a minister, have a worldwide ministry, and reach people for the Gospel.

At the same time, there are some people who are called to minister to the homeless, be a pastor in a specific community, be missionaries overseas, or just raise their families and be a blessing to those around them. There are different purposes and callings for every person. And it's up to each one of us to find out God's plan for our lives and pursue it.

A Living Sacrifice

I beseech you therefore, brethren, by the mercies of God, that ye present your bodies a living sacrifice, holy, acceptable unto God, which is your reasonable service. And be not conformed to this world: but be ye transformed by the renewing of your mind, that ye may prove what is that good, and acceptable, and perfect, will of God.

Romans 12:1-2

I was a fairly typical kid until my senior year of high school. As I neared graduation, I realized I was going to have to make decisions about my future that would determine the rest of my life. One thing I believed very strongly was that God had a plan for my life. I didn't have a clue what that plan was, but I was determined to find out! So, I started seeking the Lord.

I asked the leaders of my church, but they couldn't offer any clear direction. So, I started reading the Bible as I never had before. It was normal for me to study the Word from 9 p.m. until the wee hours of the morning throughout my senior year of high school. I had read the Bible every day of my life since I was a little kid, but I never really studied it, so I went out and bought a five-volume *Matthew Henry Commentary* to help me understand everything.

As I graduated from high school and began college, I still had no clear direction. I was a math major because that was my best subject. However, I was still seeking the Lord with all my heart for His perfect will for my life. In the middle of my first year of college, in December 1967, I came across Romans 12:1-2.

These verses changed my life. The last part of the second verse promises that I would prove the good, acceptable, and perfect will of God if I would do as instructed. That's what I wanted! I began a four-month study of what it meant to be a living sacrifice and to renew my mind. The results were more than I could have imagined.

Just four months after I got this promise from the Lord, God showed up. I had a miraculous encounter with the Lord on March 23, 1968, that I've never gotten over—and never intend to get over. God revealed Himself to me in a way that made me realize my self-righteousness was like filthy rags (Is. 64:6). But instead of striking me dead, I experienced God's unconditional love. Among the things that came out of that was a knowing that I would have a worldwide ministry someday.

God revealed His will to me, but it didn't come all at once. It came as I proved the good, acceptable, and perfect will of God. It came in stages or steps. Within the next few months, I was led to make radical decisions that set my life on a course that has brought me to where I am today.

Let Peace Rule

And let the peace of God rule in your hearts, to the which also ye are called in one body; and be ye thankful.

Colossians 3:15

Not long after I got a revelation of God's glory and His love for me, I felt like He told me to drop out of college. This was during the Vietnam War, so for me to follow God in this way meant I could be immediately drafted and sent overseas. I also stood to lose the Social Security income that I had been receiving since my father's death when I was twelve years old. I could keep this income only as long as I was still in school.

Following the Lord would cost me financially. I would also end up with a first-class ticket to a war zone where I quite possibly could have been killed. Beyond that, every person in my life whom I ever respected told me one way or another, "This isn't God." They told me that it was of the devil.

It seemed like everyone was telling me what a dunce I was and how I shouldn't be going against the way things were always done. I wasn't trying to rebel against the advice of well-meaning people, but even leaders in my church told me I was hearing from the devil. I just wanted to be obedient to what I knew God was speaking to me in my heart.

Because of the negative reactions to my desire to leave school, I backed off for a while. During that time, I was absolutely miserable. This continued for two months until I couldn't take it anymore. One night, the Lord finally spoke to me through Romans 14:23, which says, "*Whatsoever is not of faith is sin.*"

I realized I was in sin because of indecision. I determined to make a faith decision that night and stick with it. As I prayed and studied the Word for guidance, I found Colossians 3:15. The Greek word translated "*rule*" there also means to "umpire," like in a baseball game.[2]

The Lord spoke to me that I was to head in the direction that gave me the most peace. To be honest, I didn't have total peace in any direction, but just as an umpire has to make a decision and stick with it, I needed to make the call. I had the most peace about quitting school, so I stepped out of indecision and into faith to the best of my understanding.

Within twenty-four hours the Lord gave me such confirmation and joy that I have never doubted the wisdom of that decision since. That one decision, possibly more than any other, set my life on a course that has brought me to where I am today. If I had listened to all those other people, and not obeyed God, you may have never heard of me. I made it only because I valued the Lord over the opinions of everyone else in my life.

Renew Your Mind

When I served in the Army, it seemed like I only heard one good thing from a chaplain the whole time I was there. Most of the chaplains I had weren't even born again. But the day we got our orders to go to Vietnam, there was a chaplain who really blessed me.

Once we got the news about going overseas, grown men began to cry. It was a tragic situation, so this chaplain came in to console everybody. He said that the military and its experiences, including Vietnam, would be like a fire. "It will melt you," this chaplain said. "But you get to choose the mold you're poured into." What he said turned out to be a true statement.

Because I had already set my heart on the Lord, I was determined that I was going to go all the way for Him. All the pressures and the horror I went through drove me that much more toward God.

I had this miraculous encounter with the Lord, but I didn't know everything I know now. I also hadn't yet prayed in tongues or learned about the power it would release in my life (more on that later). So, I just stuck my nose in the Bible. I would read the Word of God every day, sometimes up to fifteen hours in one day.

I renewed my mind to the Word of God, and it just transformed my life (Rom. 12:2). When I came back from Vietnam, I was stronger than ever! I was walking with God, the joy of the Lord was in my heart, and I was a thousand miles farther along in my Christian walk.

You may not be a soldier in the midst of a war zone, but you will have things come against you in this life that will melt you. However, you can choose whether you'll be like the other people who become negative, bitter, and unforgiving. You can choose whether you'll murmur and complain or let these things drive you to the Lord and make you stronger and more stable in your commitment to Him.

In other words, it's your choice whether you become bitter or better. But how do you make that choice?

The Greek word rendered "*transformed*" in Romans 12:2 is *metamorphoo*.[3] It's the word from which we derive our English word metamorphosis. A little caterpillar spins a cocoon and then, after time, turns into a beautiful butterfly. If you want to be transformed from something creepy, crawly, and earthbound into something beautiful that can fly, you need to be transformed by the renewing of your mind.

You Choose

I call heaven and earth to record this day against you, that I have set before you life and death, blessing and cursing: therefore choose life, that both thou and thy seed may live.

Deuteronomy 30:19

Even though I knew God had a purpose for my life, it did not mean His will automatically came to pass. I had to choose to pursue it and be obedient to His call.

There are a lot of people who think their lives are like a pinball machine. They're just launched out there and bounce from one thing to another. They don't believe they can know God's will for their lives. They feel like they don't have any purpose, and they never fulfill their calling.

When I've ministered on things like this in my meetings, I'll ask the audience, "How many of you do not know for sure what God has called you to do?" It's not unusual for most of the people in a crowd of born-again Christians to raise their hands.

There are a lot of people who believe God is the author of whatever happens, and that He controls everything. They have this fatalistic attitude—as the song says, "*Que sera, sera.* Whatever will be, will be."

Many people have this idea that God is sovereign—that He is in control of everything that happens in their lives, good or bad. Now, I'll agree that God is sovereign if you go by the understanding that He is first in rank, order, or authority. But that does not mean He controls everything. That is not what the Word of God teaches.

You can't be passive. You are not a chess piece that just gets moved around without your consent. He has a perfect plan for every person (Jer. 29:11), but He doesn't make you walk that path. You have the ability to choose. He has even told you what the right choices are (Deut. 30:19), but He doesn't make those choices for you. It's only when you eliminate the thinking that says, "God is in control of everything," and choose to pursue God's will for your life that you'll begin to see it come to pass.

I believe the extreme "sovereignty of God" teaching is the worst doctrine in the church today. I know that's a shocking statement, but the way sovereignty is typically taught is a real faith killer. The belief that God controls everything that happens to us is one of the devil's biggest inroads into our lives. If this belief is true, then our actions are irrelevant, and our efforts are meaningless.

Second Peter 3:9 clearly states it is the Lord's will that everyone be saved, yet they aren't because He gave us a free will. It was the Lord's will for the Israelites to enter into the Promised Land shortly after their exodus from Egypt, but it took forty years for them to arrive. They delayed God's will through their disobedience. The Lord has a perfect plan for each of us, but He gives us total control over whether or not we follow His plan.

Holy Dissatisfaction

Delight thyself also in the Lord; and he shall give thee the desires of thine heart.

Psalm 37:4

Before you truly pursue God's will, you've got to become dissatisfied with where you are in life. As long as you can live without knowing God's purpose for your life, you will. You need a holy dissatisfaction with your circumstances. It's one of the ways that God reveals how He is leading you.

I remember early in our ministry when Jamie and I were pastoring a church in Seagoville, Texas. We never had a large group there. We struggled financially, and it was hard on us, yet we stayed there for two years. I had friends who asked, "Why don't you leave this place? Why don't you go where people want you?" But I just loved being in Seagoville.

I remember being at our church building one day and praying. When I looked out of the windows, it was as if everything I saw went from color to black and white. It went from being something that I liked to just being drab. I remember looking out of the windows and thinking, *This is the dinkiest town. Who would live in this place?*

All of a sudden, my love and desire to be in Seagoville changed. It was so dramatic that I thought, *God, what's going on?* I prayed for about two hours. Eventually, the Lord spoke to me and told me that on November 1, I was to leave Seagoville. At that time, God didn't tell me where I was supposed to go, but He just told me it was time for a change.

The way the Lord showed me was by changing my desires. I had a holy dissatisfaction. I didn't desire to be in Seagoville any longer. I knew that God wanted me to move on. But then I thought, *How am I going to break this to Jamie?* So, I prayed about it for a long time.

When I got home, there was a "For Sale" sign in our yard that wasn't there when I left earlier that day. I asked Jamie, "What happened?" She said, "The landlord came by and said they're selling our house, and we've got to be out on November 1." That was the exact date that God had given me, so it was a confirmation. There was a change taking place in my life and one of the ways that I discovered it was because I just knew in my spirit that there was something more.

Even though I loved the people of Seagoville, I loved the Lord first. Years before, I had learned to delight myself in Him. And because of that, He changed, or gave me, the desires of my heart.

The Desires of Your Heart

I was brought up in a legalistic church. When they taught about finding God's will, they actually said, "Whatever you want, do the exact opposite, and that will be God."

Now, if you are sincerely seeking God's will for your life, I don't recommend following that advice. But this is true for carnal Christians—people who make satisfying their own needs the greatest priority in their lives. People who don't pursue a relationship with God after they are born again can't trust their desires.

Anyone who is just waiting on heaven might be saved, but they are stuck living by their carnal nature. Those believers can't trust the desires of their hearts to be godly. However, everyone who is truly committed to God can be led by the desires of their heart. But you have to let the Lord place His desires there (Ps. 37:4).

For instance, I never wanted a Bible school. A lot of people asked me to start one, but I never wanted to, largely because I had met too many Bible school graduates who really annoyed me. They were puffed up with knowledge. But that didn't mean they had a better relationship with God or that they loved Him more than other Christians they looked down on.

I didn't want to be associated with something like that, so I had no desire to start a Bible school even though I have always had a strong desire to disciple people. But in the summer of 1993, I was in Britain and heard a man say that if you aren't training up people to do what God has shown you, you're a failure. In other words, discipling others is essential; it is not optional.

You see, it doesn't matter if you reach a million people for Christ. Your time on earth is limited. So, unless you can take what is in you and reproduce it in other people, ultimately you have failed. Your ministry will die with you. That's part of the reason why Christians are supposed to make disciples and not just converts.

I knew those things were true, so it stirred something in me when I heard someone else preach about it. I thought, *God, how can I equip believers to help them start walking in the abundant life You have made available?* The Lord answered, "A Bible school."

God showed me a different way to approach Bible school, and in that one ministry meeting, the desires of my heart changed completely. I went from being totally opposed to having a Bible school to being really excited about the idea. Charis Bible College grew from the desire God planted in my heart that day, and its influence has been growing ever since.

Steps and Stages

For the earth bringeth forth fruit of herself; first the blade, then the ear, after that the full corn in the ear.

Mark 4:28

Many people have some revelation of what the Lord wants them to do, but very few are depending on God to accomplish it. They get a word from God and make a paragraph out of it. They lean on their own understanding and often make a royal mess of things.

I remember a man who came to me with an idea for a youth center in Colorado Springs. He had heard a message about reaching out to youth, and it really got his attention. So, he found this empty retail building, which would've cost about $2 million to purchase. Then he estimated it would cost upward of another $3 million to renovate.

This man was planning to put in a skate park and other features that would draw teenagers. While they were there, he would minister to them. It was a great idea, and he had put a lot of time and effort into creating a proposal that he brought to me, hoping I would endorse it. The proposal was full of facts and figures, talking about crime among youth and other things—to help justify the need for a Christian youth center in the city.

Then I started asking this man questions. "Have you ever taught a Bible study? Have you ever worked in a youth group? Have you ever dealt with youth?" And he answered, "No," each time. It turns out, he had never done any ministry work. So, I said, "It's a great idea, but it won't work for you."

"Why not?" he asked. And then he tried to justify his plans according to the need. He referred again to all the statistics in his proposal. I didn't dispute there was a need, but I told him, "You have never been used a little bit, so you aren't going to be used a lot. It's first the blade, then the ear, and then the full corn in the ear."

This man wanted all the fruit of a harvest without going through seed and time (Gen. 8:22). God's will for your life doesn't come to pass automatically or even immediately. For you to go from zero to a thousand miles an hour instantly isn't acceleration—*it's a wreck!* There is a growth process.

I've just learned that nobody ever goes from never having done anything to being a great success. God may not be giving you an opportunity to influence more people right now because you're not ready—you're not mature enough—and He doesn't want you or anyone else to get hurt. There is first a blade, then the ear, then the full corn in the ear.

Exercise Patience

For ye have need of patience, that, after ye have done the will of God, ye might receive the promise.

Hebrews 10:36

We need to know not only God's will but also His plan for accomplishing His will. That takes time, effort, and maturity. Preparation time is never wasted time. Proper preparation will save you time in the long run.

Then we must add patience to our faith in order to fulfill God's will (James 1:4). Anyone can start a race, but not everyone crosses the finish line. Certainly, not everyone wins the race. It takes a combination of many things in order to finish well.

The human tendency is to quit, fail, and give up. Most people don't want to wait. It's not human nature to wait. The strongest, best, and most fit of all are going to fail. In our own selves, we don't have what it takes to overcome. God, on the other hand, doesn't get weary. God doesn't faint (Is. 40:28-31). He never gives up. Patience is a God quality, not a human quality. That's why it's a fruit of the Spirit (Gal. 5:22–23). Only through God can we obtain patience and endurance.

Sometimes when I teach this at Charis Bible College, people get upset. Some people have the attitude that they don't need to wait because they think God is going to do things for them instantly. I remember this one man at our Bible college who was very passionate about evangelism. He believed the Lord showed him that he would lead one million people to receive the Gospel.

I was teaching in one of my classes about these things, and this man stood up and rebuked me! He talked about all the people who needed to hear the Gospel and said, "I need to be out there ministering! I can't wait!" Now, part of what he was saying is true. People do need to hear the Gospel. But he also needed time to prepare himself so he could share that message with people over the long haul.

This man ended up quitting school because he was so adamant about needing to do something right away. That's been more than twenty years ago. I don't know if he's making any impact for the kingdom of God, but if he would have brought a million people to Christ, I likely would have heard about it! He certainly would have been better off being patient and letting God work in his life to prepare him for his ministry.

We first must believe, then act, and then be patient before we receive the full manifestation of what we believe for. We can only bring forth fruit with patience (Luke 8:15). Patience is what makes us perfect and complete (James 1:4). Patience comes through Scripture (Rom. 15:4). Patience is simply faith over a prolonged period of time.

A Place Called There

And the word of the LORD came unto him, saying, Get thee hence, and turn thee eastward, and hide thyself by the brook Cherith, that is before Jordan. And it shall be, that thou shalt drink of the brook; and I have commanded the ravens to feed thee there.

1 Kings 17:2–4

God doesn't reveal His complete plan immediately. He reveals His will to us one step at a time. After we obey the first step, He shows us the next one. Elijah had obeyed the first thing the Lord told him to do by going boldly to Ahab and predicting a drought (1 Kgs. 17:1). He didn't get this second word from the Lord about his provision until he had obeyed the first word.

Why should the Lord show us step two or ten if we haven't obeyed step one? That would just make us more accountable. So, don't try to figure out the next step until you have acted on what you know to do right now. That's a powerful truth.

The Lord told the prophet Elijah to go to the brook Cherith. He had already commanded the ravens to bring Elijah bread and meat "*there*" every morning and evening. This was miraculous! But notice, the Lord didn't send Elijah's provision to where he was. A quarterback doesn't throw the football to where the receiver is, but to where the receiver is going. Elijah's miracle wasn't where he was but where the Lord was leading him.

Each of us has a place called "there," where the blessings of the Lord are waiting. The Lord never fails to provide, but people often fail to receive because they aren't all there! If Elijah had not gone to his place called "there," his disobedience would not have stopped God's faithfulness. But he would not have received the provision. It was over there, by the brook Cherith.

This is exactly what is happening to many Christians who are seeking God's will for their lives. They may know God's will, but if they aren't obedient and in their place called "there," they won't see God's provision.

Over the years, I've heard many people say the Lord told them to attend Charis Bible College, but they just can't see how it could happen, typically when it comes to finances. They want to see the Lord's provision before they commit, especially before moving their family. But that's not how it works.

Some of you are not seeing God's provision because you aren't doing what He has told you to do. This doesn't mean the Lord is punishing you. But if Elijah hadn't gone "there," he would have never received his provision. The Lord has provision for you too, but it's "there." This is why, when people visit our Charis campus in Woodland Park, Colorado, we have a big green-and-yellow sign just inside the gates that says, "Welcome to your place called 'there.'"

I could tell you many stories of people who left behind homes, careers, and other things because they believed God had called them to attend Charis. And once they arrived at their place called "there"—once they took that first step—that's where they found jobs, homes, and even spouses! Where God guides, He provides!

Course Correction

For the gifts and calling of God are *without repentance.*

Romans 11:29

God doesn't change. Whatever His purpose for your life was when He created you, that hasn't changed either. You might be a long way from where God wants you to be right now, but God can get you where you need to be.

Modern technology allows you to have a global positioning system (GPS) in your car to help you find your way around town. GPS devices even speak to you and tell you where to turn. But when you are driving somewhere and make a wrong turn, the GPS doesn't freak out and say, "You missed it! You'll never get there now!" No, if you make a wrong turn, the GPS says, "Recalculating."

It refigures your directions and tells you what to do next to get where you need to go; it will still get you to your destination. Missing a turn doesn't mean you need to give up and go home. God is at least as good as a GPS. It doesn't matter where you are—God can recalculate. God can take what you have done and figure a way to get you back on track. You can still get where God planned for you to go.

Years ago, I had the chance to meet astronaut Jim Irwin when we were being interviewed on the same television program. Afterward, I asked him a bunch of questions about landing on the moon because I had been serving in Vietnam when a lot of those space missions happened.

One of the things he shared really blessed me. He said that people think the rocket launched their capsule into space and they just made a beeline to the moon. But it wasn't that way. That thing continually got off course. Periodically, these astronauts had to report their position, get calculations to fix their trajectory, and fire their engines for a few moments to straighten out. This is how they traveled all the way to the moon!

Instead of a straight line, their capsule went all over the place during their journey. Jim even used his hand to illustrate a zig-zag pattern to show how they went. He said they used a series of course corrections to reach their destination.

There was also a 500-mile-wide area that NASA had planned for the lunar module's landing. By the time they reached the moon's surface, Jim said they ended up landing within five feet of missing that huge area. That's just amazing!

That's kind of like how our lives are. The gifts and the calling of God never change. You may have made some wrong turns in your life, but God's will for you has not changed. He still has a plan for you. Even if you have made a royal mess of your life, God can take what you have done and cause it to work together for good (Rom. 8:28). He will get you where you need to be if you will be sensitive to His course corrections!

TIMING IS EVERYTHING

And seeing one of them suffer wrong, [Moses] defended him, and avenged him that was oppressed, and smote the Egyptian: for he supposed his brethren would have understood how that God by his hand would deliver them: but they understood not.

Acts 7:24–25

Stephen was the first Christian martyr. Right before he was stoned to death, he recounted Jewish history to the council to show that he wasn't against the Jewish faith. He recounted the promises and prophecies that were given to the Jews about the coming of the Messiah. Stephen was speaking under the inspiration of the Holy Spirit when he said, "*it came into* [Moses'] *heart to visit his brethren the children of Israel*" (Acts 7:23).

Moses knew God had called him to deliver Israel but thought that it was going to happen by killing an Egyptian. He thought the Jews would recognize how God had anointed him to rescue them. As a result, he totally missed

God's timing and plan for bringing it to pass. His mistake cost him forty years in the wilderness and the Israelites thirty years of extra bondage that God never intended.

You see, God had told Abraham that the children of Israel would be sojourners in a foreign land for 400 years (Gen. 15:13). And that period didn't refer to just the slavery in Egypt, but the total years from when God made the promise. The Apostle Paul wrote that the Law came 430 years after the promise (Gal. 3:17).

The day Moses led the Israelites out of Egypt was the end of the 430 years (Ex. 12:40). So, if you subtract the forty years that Moses spent in the wilderness, you'll see that he was ten years premature in trying to bring about what God had put in his heart. This is an important piece of information we should learn from (1 Cor. 10:11).

God's will for your life involves His timing. His plans can't be sped up. But you *can* delay God's will from coming to pass—Moses delayed it thirty years. It isn't hard to imagine Moses thinking he could free the Israelites based on his own power and influence, having been raised in Pharaoh's household. But God was going to do it in a miraculous way so there would be no mistaking Who saved them (Ex. 3:7–22).

A lot of Christians today take the same approach to God's will as Moses did. They think, *Okay, God, I can handle it from here. You just get me introduced, put me on the stage, and I'll do the rest*. A person may discover God's will for their lives, but then they will try to build God's kingdom in their own ability and timing. This is causing tremendous problems in the body of Christ.

God will call you to do something that is absolutely beyond your natural ability. He wants to do things in a supernatural way that testifies of His glory. God uses people to do things beyond their ability (1 Cor. 1:26–30), so when others see it, they say, "Wow! That had to be God!"

Your Spirit Knows

But God hath revealed them *unto us by his Spirit: for the Spirit searcheth all things, yea, the deep things of God.*

1 Corinthians 2:10

Unless we know how to draw out the wisdom and power of God from our spirit, we will end up trying to discern God's will by judging our circumstances. King David wrote that no one should be like a horse or mule, which has no understanding and must be led around by bit and bridle

(Ps. 32:8–9). We are supposed to be led by God and not our circumstances.

If you are a Christian, your born-again spirit knows everything you need to know. You already have wisdom in your spirit. God understands that we live in a physical world and the Scripture says that if any man lacks wisdom let him ask God (James 1:5). But the wisdom we receive doesn't come from heaven.

God has already abounded toward us in all wisdom and prudence (Eph. 1:8). The Bible says that we have a special anointing, or unction, from God and our spirit knows all things (1 John 2:20). Our job is to draw out what God has already put in us.

Isaiah prophesied that we would hear a voice behind us saying, "*This is the way, walk ye in it,*" (Is. 30:21). We should be led by the still small voice of God (1 Kgs. 19:12–13). Allowing our circumstances to dictate our course of action is no different than a mule being pulled this way and that way by a bit.

One night, the Apostle Paul had a dream of a man from Macedonia calling him over to help them (Acts 16:9). When he woke up in the morning, he knew that dream meant that God was sending him to minister to the people of Macedonia. So, Paul and Silas traveled to Macedonia and entered the city of Philippi.

Within days they were arrested, beaten, and locked in the lowest part of the dungeon (Acts 16:23–24). In similar circumstances, I think most of us would think, *Well, this must not have been God*. We would reason that God would never lead us to do something that would land us in jail. But circumstances are not a reliable indicator of God's will.

Paul was following God's leading and going to Philippi was exactly what God told him to do. So, at midnight, Paul and Silas started singing and praising God (Acts 16:25–34). Then the Lord got to tapping His foot, all the doors of the prison opened, and Paul and Silas got the jailer and his household saved!

Observing circumstances is not an accurate way to discern God's will. The spirit on the inside of us knows all things. Part of following God's will involves learning to listen to the voice of God inside of us and obeying no matter what. In our spirit, we have supernatural God-ordained wisdom; by tapping into it, we will begin to see things that are hidden to our natural mind.

Unravel the Mystery

For he that speaketh in an unknown *tongue speaketh not unto men, but unto God: for no man understandeth him; howbeit in the spirit he speaketh mysteries.*

1 Corinthians 14:2

This scripture is part of the same letter in which the Apostle Paul said, "*We speak the wisdom of God in a mystery*" (1 Cor. 2:6–7). In this verse, he says that when you are speaking in tongues, you are speaking mysteries.

Paul was a man who helped change the world. It was said of him that he was among those who "*turned the world upside down*" (Acts 17:6). He wrote almost half of the New Testament. Do you know when he received all that wisdom? When he was born again!

God put His supernatural wisdom in Paul's born-again spirit. Just as any other believer, Paul had an unction (anointing) from the Holy One and he knew all things (1 John 2:20)—he had the mind of Christ (1 Cor. 2:16). Paul says that he drew the knowledge out of his spirit by speaking in tongues.

Even though our spirit knows all things, we still have to get the knowledge into our natural understanding. Paul said, *"If I pray in an unknown tongue, my spirit prayeth, but my understanding is unfruitful"* (1 Cor. 14:14).

When we speak in tongues, our spirit prays. Our spirit is the part of us that knows all things, is renewed in knowledge, and has the mind of Christ. This is the same part of us that always has peace and love; it doesn't have any questions or problems. Our spirit prays the hidden wisdom of God in a mystery, under the inspiration of the Holy Spirit.

One of the most important things we can do when we come up against a difficult situation is pray in tongues. Our born-again spirit prays our answer when we speak in tongues. Our spirit prays the wisdom we need and gives us instruction. Scripture says that when we speak in tongues, our understanding is unfruitful. In other words, our mind doesn't understand what we are saying. But Paul tells us how to unravel the mystery:

> *Wherefore let him that speaketh in an* unknown *tongue pray that he may interpret.*
>
> 1 Corinthians 14:13

We are speaking the hidden wisdom of God when we pray in tongues. It isn't gibberish; it's just that our mind doesn't understand spiritual things. As we pray, the wisdom of God comes right out of our mouths. It comes out in a language we don't understand; we just need to get an interpretation.

Speaking in tongues is like flipping a supernatural switch—we turn on a powerful generator and the life and wisdom of God that is in our spirit starts coming out of our mouth. All we have to do is ask God to give us an interpretation of what we are praying from our spirit, and He will reveal to us the wisdom we are speaking in tongues.

GET THE INTERPRETATION

Many years ago, our Charis Bible College was in a period of significant growth. So much so that it was outgrowing the 14,600-square-foot facility in Colorado Springs that housed our ministry, television studio, and school.

In time, we actually ended up finding a building that was 110,000 square feet, but only part of it could be used for office space. We had to build out the rest of it for our ministry and Bible college. It was estimated that the renovations on the building would cost $3.2 million, and that was on top of the purchase price of $3.25 million, which was a big step for us at the time.

After we purchased the building, we tried to obtain a construction loan for the renovations. Initially, the lender guaranteed us the construction loan. They said, "We wouldn't give you a loan for the building if we weren't planning to give you the construction loan." But for nine months, we waited. And every time we asked our banker about the loan, he kept telling us we would get it "next week." It was a difficult situation, and we needed to do something, but they just wouldn't give us the money.

Finally, the banker said, "We'll just get a new appraisal and start the whole process over." All I could see was another nine months of delays. Something didn't seem right, so I committed to specifically set aside time with the Lord to pray.

At the time, we lived on property with miles of trails that I had personally built. I took a walk down one of them and prayed in tongues to seek an interpretation. I wasn't a hundred yards down that trail before the Lord brought to remembrance some things that were spoken to me two years earlier. Someone had given me a prophecy that I wouldn't need to take out a loan because I already had my own bank.

When the Holy Spirit brought that to my remembrance (John 14:26), I thought, *I have my own bank? Where is it?* Then I recalled the rest of the prophecy—my ministry partners would be my bank! Somehow or another I hadn't associated the prophecy with the building program.

Believing that it was the Lord who brought that prophecy back to my memory through praying in tongues and asking for an interpretation, I refused to pursue a loan any further and decided that I would get all the money from my partners. That looked impossible at the time. It had taken us over a decade to save $30,000. At that rate, I would have been over 120 years old when the $3.2 million came in.

Fourteen months later, we had that $3.2 million, the building was finished, and we moved in without the debt of a construction loan. It was one of the best decisions I have ever made. Over the years, I've discovered that God will show me solutions or answers through praying in tongues and interpretation.

When you pray in tongues, it's your spirit praying. Your spirit has been born again, has the mind of Christ (1 Cor. 2:16), and knows exactly what to do. It has an unction from God so that you know all things (1 John 2:20). If you could walk in the power and revelation of your spirit, it would transform your physical life and help you fulfill God's will in your life.

Don't Quit

I can do all things through Christ which strengtheneth me.

Philippians 4:13

I consider the joy and peace I have in the Lord to be two of my greatest assets. I'm not struggling to accomplish God's will. In fact, although we are reaching farther with the Gospel than ever before and have more demands on our time and resources than ever before, I'm doing it with less effort than ever before. I believe that's the way it's supposed to be. We should build up momentum as we go through life. It shouldn't take the same or greater effort the longer we live.

There is a right and wrong way to run our race, and I feel that most of the hurt and pain we suffer is self-inflicted. Of course, we have an enemy who is seeking to destroy our lives. But we have a Friend who is with us every step of the way, giving us supernatural strength (Gal. 2:20).

As I mentioned before, I used to run sprints on the track team in high school, then they moved me to a cross-country race. They wanted me to run for miles when I was used to running up to 440 yards. As a result, in my first race, I took off like a rabbit. I was ahead of everyone.

But about the half-mile mark, I was pretty much done. Everyone passed me and I came in dead last. I learned it's easy to start, but it takes a lot more to finish well.

In my life, I've really come to admire people who finish strong. I tend to gravitate toward people who've been in the ministry for a long time and maintained their faith and joy. One of those people is Pastor Bob Nichols.

Early on in my ministry, I went to a conference at Calvary Cathedral in Fort Worth, Texas, where Bob Nichols was the pastor. All of the big-name ministers at the time were there, prophesying to each other, getting all kinds of awesome words from the Lord.

I remember sitting in that huge auditorium full of people, feeling so small and insignificant. During the song service, they said, "Go around and greet someone," but that whole time, I was thinking, *God, I need help. I need somebody to encourage me.*

Pastor Bob somehow saw me, got off the platform, pushed his way through all those people, and started hugging me. Pastor Bob started saying, "Brother, I love you, and God loves you. Don't quit! Hold on!" He just held on to me and ministered to me. Then, he went back up to the front of the auditorium.

Pastor Bob saw something in me that only God could see. I had this vision of touching the whole world with the Gospel, but here I was feeling small and insignificant. What Pastor Bob did lit a fire under me, and I was able to hold on to that vision.

Keep At It

And we desire that every one of you do shew the same diligence to the full assurance of hope unto the end: that ye be not slothful, but followers of them who through faith and patience inherit the promises.

Hebrews 6:11–12

Abraham had to patiently endure to inherit the promise God made to him. God made a promise to Abraham that he would be the father of many nations. Abraham had faith in what he heard.

Faith comes by hearing and hearing by the Word of God (Rom. 10:17). Abraham had a promise that he anchored his faith to, and after he had patiently endured, he obtained the promise (Heb. 6:13–15). But it took a long time.

Abraham was about eighty-six years old when God promised him that his descendants would outnumber the stars in the sky (Gen. 15:4–5), but his son Isaac wasn't born until he was 100 years old (Gen. 21:5). How many of us would have waited on a promise that long? Most people think God didn't come through for them unless something happens within the first five seconds of praying.

We need to realize that it often takes time to see God's will come to pass. Trying to find, follow, and fulfill God's will for your life is a process. Remember, God can't just take you from where you are to where you are supposed to be all in one step.

The Lord spoke to me on July 26, 1999, and told me I was just then beginning my ministry. Now, that was discouraging and encouraging all at the same time. I had been pursuing God's will for my life since 1968, and here I was, more than thirty years into ministry, and the Lord said I was just beginning.

He said if I had died or quit before going on television on January 3, 2000, I would have missed His will for my life. It's not that I had been out of the will of God; I had just been in preparation for all those years. I was just entering into His perfect will (Rom. 12:2).

Then, the Lord spoke to me on January 31, 2002, and told me I was limiting Him by my small thinking. When I changed my thinking, the results were miraculous. We had about thirty employees at the time, now we have over 1,200. At that time, we were reaching a small percentage of the United States with our *Gospel Truth* television program; now we can reach a potential audience of 6 billion people worldwide and have our own television network. We have $150 million worth of debt-free buildings on our Charis campus and are in the middle of a $1 billion expansion plan.

This all started happening more than thirty years after I entered into ministry. I'm fulfilling God's will step by step. It takes time so we need to have patience to not give up along the way.

Run Your Race

I have fought a good fight, I have finished my course, I have kept the faith.

2 Timothy 4:7

Many people start their race in life well but don't have the stamina to finish. Everywhere I go, I talk to people who have basically left the race or are just walking now—plodding along with no hope of winning. Anybody can start strong, but I really admire those who finish strong.

I've heard that eighty percent of all people who enter the ministry quit within five years.[4] And of the twenty percent who stay, eighty percent are nearing burnout.[5] That means only four percent of ministers last more than five years and are still thriving, instead of just surviving. That's a terrible statistic, but I can believe it's true. I've seen countless ministers come and go and others struggle just to keep their noses above water.

But these things are not exclusive to ministers. When you pursue what God has called you to do in ministry, business, government, or some other area, there will be resistance. If you are not experiencing some kind of resistance in your life, it may be that you and the devil are heading in the same direction!

When God calls you to do something and you follow through and start doing it, it's like Satan draws a big target on your back. That's especially true the farther you go in pursuing God's will. That's why it's so important to have a strong relationship with God.

I knew a pastor who loved the Lord and saw miracles happen in his ministry. But at some point, some negative things happened, and he got down on himself. He began entertaining negative thoughts and giving in to discouragement. In the process, he got so mad at God that he drove down the street, threw his Bible out the window, and went and took drugs because that's what he did before he was born again. He ended up overdosing and nearly died!

Later, when I went to see him in the psych ward of the hospital, he said, "I thought I was more mature than this. How could a person who loved God, witnessed for Him, and been a pastor do something like this?"

I told him that following the Lord is like flying in an airplane. It's not you that is flying at 35,000 feet and going 500 miles an hour. It's the plane. It's only your position in the plane that allows you to do that. You step out of the plane, and you'll sink like a rock. All you did was step out of your dependence on the Lord, and your flesh went back to what it was used to.

This is not how it has to be. The Lord not only calls us but also equips us to do His will. There is a way to finish our course with joy (Acts 20:24). But it's not going to happen automatically. We live in a fallen world. Things go from good to bad, order to disorder. Left alone, nothing gets better on its own. It takes constant attention to keep a house up, a car running, our yards groomed, and our lives on track. There is a biblical way to finish strong.

Keep Your Eyes on Jesus

Better is the end of a thing than the beginning thereof: and *the patient in spirit is better than the proud in spirit.*

Ecclesiastes 7:8

When I was a kid, I would mow our yard back and forth in long straight rows. I wanted it to look really sharp. The way I did it was by picking an object in front of me and mowing straight for it. If I tried to do a straight row by looking down at the grass in front of the mower, it would be crooked every single time.

Hebrews 12:1–2 says, "*Let us run with patience the race that is set before us, looking unto Jesus the author and finisher of our faith.*" This is the way you would run a race. You can't just look right in front of your feet, or you'll run all over the track. You also can't look at the other runners or the people in the grandstands. You'll get distracted. If you're going to finish the race and fulfill God's will, you have to look to Jesus and stay focused on Him.

It says in Hebrews 12:3 that you have to "*consider him that endured such contradiction of sinners against himself, lest ye be wearied and faint in your minds.*" The real battle is right between your ears! Nothing external can defeat you.

I know that's a statement many people wouldn't agree with. They think, *You don't understand. I've got this financial problem. I've got this relational problem. I have to give up. I don't have any choice.* But you always have a choice to believe God! Really, what defeats you is how you think about those things. That's where it starts.

Everybody wants the testimony, but nobody wants the test! You can quit when things get hard, and most people wouldn't disapprove. They'd only say something if you *don't* act that way. They'd get mad at you when you start saying you can overcome in every situation. They believe you should be preparing for the worst. They want to pull you down to their level instead of rising to the level of faith you are trying to walk in.

The reason you must look to Jesus is because it's in your mind that you faint. If you've started to follow God's will but now you've come up against something that looks impossible, the way you think will determine whether you experience victory or whether you quit. Are you going to be overcome by circumstances? Are you going to let them defeat and discourage you? None of these things can destroy you unless you get weary and faint in your mind.

I'll tell you, if you are going to fulfill God's will, you're going to have to adopt these attitudes I'm talking about. You have to determine that you will finish strong. It's only after you finish your course with joy that you realize all the benefits.

Conclusion

God created us to be so much more than what most of us are experiencing. Find the purpose God has for you. Seek the Lord and learn to hear His voice. Then set a goal and do something constructive with your life.

You may not fulfill God's plan for your life overnight, but if you start taking steps you will get there. I tell people that I may not have arrived, but I've left. You just have to be patient. If you miss God on something, it may take Him some time to get you back on track and heading in the right direction. But if you make seeking God your lifestyle, things will work out.

Live your life so that when you are gone, people are going to miss you. You will have to leave the safety and security the world offers and take some chances, but that's why God sent the Holy Spirit to help you. Unless you are living on the edge, you're taking up too much space. So, get out there and discover God's will for your life and be a blessing. You won't regret it!

FURTHER STUDY

If you enjoyed this booklet and would like to learn more about some of the things I've shared, I suggest my teachings:

- Ten Godly Leadership Essentials
- Excellence: How to Pursue an Excellent Spirit
- How to Prepare Your Heart
- Lessons from Elijah
- My Appointment with God

These teachings are available for free at **awmi.net**, or they can be purchased at **awmi.net/store**.

Receive Jesus as Your Savior

Choosing to receive Jesus Christ as your Lord and Savior is the most important decision you'll ever make!

God's Word promises, *"That if thou shalt confess with thy mouth the Lord Jesus, and shalt believe in thine heart that God hath raised him from the dead, thou shalt be saved. For with the heart man believeth unto righteousness; and with the mouth confession is made unto salvation"* (Rom. 10:9–10). *"For whosoever shall call upon the name of the Lord shall be saved"* (Rom. 10:13). By His grace, God has already done everything to provide salvation. Your part is simply to believe and receive.

Pray out loud: "Jesus, I acknowledge that I've sinned and need to receive what you did for the forgiveness of my sins. I confess that You are my Lord and Savior. I believe in my heart that God raised You from the dead. By faith in Your Word, I receive salvation now. Thank You for saving me."

The very moment you commit your life to Jesus Christ, the truth of His Word instantly comes to pass in your spirit. Now that you're born again, there's a brand-new you!

Please contact us and let us know that you've prayed to receive Jesus as your Savior. We'd like to send you some free materials to help you on your new journey. Call our Helpline: **719-635-1111** (available 24 hours a day, seven days a week) to speak to a staff member who is here to help you understand and grow in your new relationship with the Lord.

Welcome to your new life!

Receive the Holy Spirit

As His child, your loving heavenly Father wants to give you the supernatural power you need to live a new life. *"For every one that asketh receiveth; and he that seeketh findeth; and to him that knocketh it shall be opened…how much more shall* your *heavenly Father give the Holy Spirit to them that ask him?"* (Luke 11:10–13).

All you have to do is ask, believe, and receive! Pray this: "Father, I recognize my need for Your power to live a new life. Please fill me with Your Holy Spirit. By faith, I receive it right now. Thank You for baptizing me. Holy Spirit, You are welcome in my life."

Some syllables from a language you don't recognize will rise up from your heart to your mouth (1 Cor. 14:14). As you speak them out loud by faith, you're releasing God's power from within and building yourself up in the spirit (1 Cor. 14:4). You can do this whenever and wherever you like.

It doesn't really matter whether you felt anything or not when you prayed to receive the Lord and His Spirit. If you believed in your heart that you received, then God's Word promises you did. *"Therefore I say unto you, What things soever ye desire, when ye pray, believe that ye receive* them, *and ye shall have* them" (Mark 11:24). God always honors His Word—believe it!

We would like to rejoice with you, pray with you, and answer any questions to help you understand more fully what has taken place in your life!

Please contact us to let us know that you've prayed to be filled with the Holy Spirit and to request the book *The New You & the Holy Spirit*. This book will explain in more detail about the benefits of being filled with the Holy Spirit and speaking in tongues. Call our Helpline: **719-635-1111** (available 24 hours a day, seven days a week).

Endnotes

1. Nicole Golden, "Fast-Twitch vs. Slow-Twitch Muscle Fiber Types," NASM.org, accessed September 17, 2024, https://blog.nasm.org/fitness/understanding-fast-twitch-vs-slow-twitch-mucle-fibers

2. *Thayer's Greek Lexicon*, s.v. "βραβεύω" ("brabeúō"), accessed September 13, 2024, https://www.blueletterbible.org/lexicon/g1018/kjv/tr/0-1/

3. *Strong's Definitions*, s.v. "μεταμορφόω" ("metamorphóō"), accessed September 12, 2024, https://www.blueletterbible.org/lexicon/g3339/kjv/tr/0-1/

4. Trisha R. Peach, "Burnout, Timeout, and Fallout: A Qualitative Study of Why Pastors Leave Ministry," (Doctoral thesis, Bethel University, 2022), 7, 49-50, and 134, https://spark.bethel.edu/cgi/viewcontent.cgi?article=1804&context=etd

5. James Dobson, "Pastors And Churches Are Struggling," *Apostolic Information Service*, Dec. 20, 2007, https://www.apostolic.edu/pastors-and-churches-are-struggling/

Call for Prayer

If you need prayer for any reason, you can call our Helpline, 24 hours a day, seven days a week at **719-635-1111**. A trained prayer minister will answer your call and pray with you.

Every day, we receive testimonies of healings and other miracles from our Helpline, and we are ministering God's nearly-too-good-to-be-true message of the Gospel to more people than ever. So, I encourage you to call today!

About the Author

Andrew Wommack's life was forever changed the moment he encountered the supernatural love of God on March 23, 1968. As a renowned Bible teacher and author, Andrew has made it his mission to change the way the world sees God.

Andrew's vision is to go as far and deep with the Gospel as possible. His message goes far through the *Gospel Truth* television program, which is available to over half the world's population. The message goes deep through discipleship at Charis Bible College, headquartered in Woodland Park, Colorado. Founded in 1994, Charis has campuses across the United States and around the globe.

Andrew also has an extensive library of teaching materials in print, audio, and video. More than 200,000 hours of free teachings can be accessed at **awmi.net**.

CONTACT INFORMATION

Andrew Wommack Ministries, Inc.
PO Box 3333
Colorado Springs, CO 80934-3333
info@awmi.net
awmi.net

Helpline: 719-635-1111 (available 24/7)

Charis Bible College
info@charisbiblecollege.org
844-360-9577
CharisBibleCollege.org

For a complete list of all of our offices,
visit **awmi.net/contact-us**.

Connect with us on social media.

Sign up to watch anytime, anywhere, for free.

GOSPEL TRUTH
NETWORK

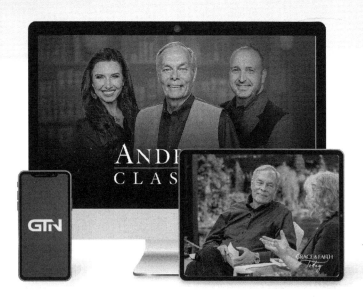

GTNTV.com

Download our apps available on mobile and TV platforms or stream GTN on Glorystar Satellite Network.